PECULIAR HONORS

Also by Sharon Cumberland

The Arithmetic of Mourning
Greatest Hits 1983-2000

PECULIAR HONORS

**Poems by
Sharon Cumberland**

*Sharon Cumberland
Seattle, 2017*

Black Heron Press
Post Office Box 13396
Mill Creek, Washington 98082
www.blackheronpress.com

ISBN 978-0-930773-99-1

The poet wishes to thank the editors of the following publications in which several of the poems appeared, some in slightly different versions: *Atlanta Review*: "Papal Tombs, Basilica of St. Peter"; *Connecticut Review*: "Annunciation"; *Contact II*: "Lipstick"; *Cortland Review*: "On Seeing Keats' Deathroom"; *Floating Bridge 2*: "At the Foot of the Great Table"; *Floating Bridge 3*: "Some Poems," "Art Collector," "On the Burke Gilman Trail," "Tacoma Screw," "Ranuccio Tomassoni," "Those Killed by Serpents," "Before They Were Men," "Report to New York," "On the Tarmac at Indianapolis," "Vista Point," "Speckled Egg," "The Man Who Wants You," "Strolling the Front at Largs," "Helium Balloons," "Rosenkavalier," "Monk's Gate," "Why I Turned Onto Iron Goat Road"; *Fresh Ground*: "The Fur-Faced Boys"; *Indiana Review*: "Postulant," "Smoke Offering"; *Image*: "Kyrie Pantokrator," "Prayer"; Iowa Review: "Ars Poetica," "Unreasonable Woman"; *Kalliope*: "Before"; *Laurel Review*: "I Know I am Capable of Great Love"; *Meridian*: "Lucidity"; *Ploughshares*: "What You Have," "On Going In," "Habit"; *Poets On*: "Final Diet"; Psychopoetica: "Schubertiad"; *Pulpsmith*: "The Arithmetic of Mourning"; *River Oak Review*: "Athena in Seattle," "Hera at the Piano"; *Roanoke Review*: "The Killing Speed"; *Verse*: "Christ Rebuked the Waves," "Yeshua Summoned the Twelve"; *Westcoast* (Glasgow): "Before"; *The Worchester Review*: "La Boheme."

"On Seeing Keats' Deathroom" incorporates the fourteen end-rhyming words of Keats' sonnet, "On Seeing the Elgin Marbles."

    Poems on the life of Yeshua incorporate the fourteen end-rhyming words of the following Shakespearean sonnets:

"Annunciation"	Sonnet 127
"The Travelers"	Sonnet 14
"Runaway"	Sonnet 12

"Marriage at Cana"	Sonnet 9
"Yeshua Summoned the Twelve"	Sonnet 91
"Yeshua Rebuked the Waves"	Sonnet 65
"Get Up, Little Girl!"	Sonnet 116

The poet wishes to thank the Corporation of Yaddo for many years of encourage-ment and support, and Seattle University for two summer writing grants.

The hymns quoted are from *The Psalms and Hymns of Isaac Watts* (George Burder, 1806).

In Memoriam
JOHN ANDREW SIMPSON
1977 - 1983

CONTENTS

PECULIAR HONORS

Let every creature rise and bring
Peculiar honors to our King.
Angels descend with songs again,
And earth repeat the long Amen.

—Isaac Watts, Hymn LXXII

SOME POEMS

are like microbes in agar nurtured
by lab-coated technicians—
magi breathing lightly
over the delicate mitosis of words.
They could cure cancer for all I know,
or grow stem cells that duplicate
the organs of creation.
But only the man in the white coat
understands, or the woman
with severe hair, who has wrapped
herself in an opera cape.
The rest of us poke our dirty fingers
in the gel, press our ears
to the Petrie dish,
or bang it against the table
like a monkey pounding
a microscope against
a tamarind tree.

CHILDREN IN SHOPPING CARTS

You see them at Wal-Mart and Costco,
sitting cross-legged in wire baskets,
turning a can of yams or green beans
in their pillowy hands, or gnawing

on a wand of string cheese. They are placid,
as in a warm tub, or dully touring
a strange culture from a safe remove.
To you they seem carefully selected

from the secret aisle, where babies wait
in sleepy ranks, and moon-faced toddlers
waddle about in a playpen, pacifiers
and price tags pinned to their pink and blue overalls.

Women who want children make their selections,
pay the price, wheel the child from the store
in a wire cart. Sometimes they cry, sometimes
they try to escape, only to be chased and claimed

by their new mothers. Yet even the stores
with generous return policies seem never
to take them back. Witness the older ones
whining to their parents up and down the aisles

for chips and sodas, forgetful of their origins:
even these retain an aboriginal ease
with their surroundings, because places of buying
and of selling are truly their native soil.

ARS POETICA

I

A young woman with orange hair,
wearing white anklets,
tight skirt
with black and red zig-zags,
is walking down Fifth Avenue.
You wouldn't know she was there
if I didn't tell you,
or about the five inch spikes
on her heels, and the tiny-footed
dog with the Chinese face she leads on a yellow string.
You wouldn't see the businessmen
swing their heads involuntarily
to see her breasts bounce
under the white-ribbed tee shirt.
"Why should I know that?" you say.
"Will it find me a job
or make my lover take me back?
Will it buy me a burger
and a big fries?"
And then I say: You ask
the wrong questions.
Better to ask:
Could you see her nipples?
Was she smiling?

II

There is a madman standing on the corner of Fifty-seventh and Fifth.
He believes he is clad in barbed wire from head to foot.

**

15

He takes tiny steps so he won't feel the barbs too deeply.
He talks funny so his cheeks won't bleed.
The people hurry by and don't look:
they have their own worries.
He cries for help, gives detailed directions to a hardware store,
but he can't move his mouth, so they don't understand
what he's shouting: "Buy me some wire clippers!
I promise to pay you back!" But only Tiffany's and Saks
and fancy shops are near—fine scissors for cutting
gold links don't work on barbed wire.
He works his way down Fifth, weeping and mumbling.
He sees a yellow string from the edge of his eye—
a dog leading a girl—neither one the type
a guy like him ever got near to,
even before—when he was young, and not wired.
"So what's the point?" you say. "Should I
be glad I'm not crazy?" I point
the way my mother taught me not to—See? See?
See him, barbed and unbarbed.

III

A man in a suit, a fine suit,
not a loud or obvious suit,
a fine stripe, but not too
dignified—just right, the suit
stripe matching the shirt stripe—
not precisely, but just enough
to look fine, clean—a stylish
combination—with French cuffs,

**

gold cufflinks and tie tack;
a rep tie with broad blue
stripe—silk, maroon background
(the tie is central—everything
depends upon the right tie);
a man in a fine suit strides
toward lunch at Rumplemeyer's.
He sees himself reflected
in the window at Tiffany's—
sees his face in the window-
dressing: Indian king, a diamond
in his forehead, gilded elephant,
mahout with a ruby prod—he likes
what he sees: his hairline
is holding its own. He smiles,
a match for the elegant crowd
around him, and the girls,
girls with circus hips that swing
like a trapeze in a Big Top:
breasts jounce and bow. There goes
a freakish dog with a spike-heeled
showgirl in the lead. There goes
a screaming Tom O'Bedlam—a side-
show for the man in a fine suit,
on a great street at lunchtime.
"OK," you say, "I see him,
and so what?" That's enough
I say. Seeing is enough.

ART COLLECTOR

He hunches in the stacks, hides *Quattro Pittori Toscani* beneath his coat.
    How they inspire him, his painters—Masaccio,
    Angelico, Masolino—with their Marys, like summoning angels.
He sits in a men's room stall, turns glossy pages, fingers the binding,
    cuts the security dot from its spine like a tumor.
    O Piero della Francesca! Free now to come home.
Downstairshechecksoutdecoys: *MuseumsoftheWorld,TheRazor'sEdge,*
    hiding treasures in his vest: angels flutter, virgins throb at his heart.
    He bears them to the street—he is their reliquary; their acolyte.
Back at his apartment, he spreads out his albums, his razor, the glue.
    How he loves angels! Michael's fiery sword,
    Gabriel's annunciating lily: "Fear not, God is with thee."
He flips the glistening pages, a fat volume of treasure.
    Mary's halos bob to and fro, fearing then facing,
    obeying the summons, as he does: *cut her out, paste her in.*
He kisses her snowy hands, rubs his cheek against her snowy skin,
    a knight in Mary's Army—her cavalier, her angel.
    O Mother! O page upon page of devotion!
He throws mutilated books in the corner as he glues.
    They flop and slide, crawling with letters like so many vermin:
    the proverbial, worthless, thousand words.

ON THE BURKE GILMAN TRAIL

They're not wearing underwear, you know,
those serious bikers with their muscled calves
and rock-solid bottoms: their cycling pants
have chamois crotches to ease the friction
of the saddle on their privates. Imagine
the shaggy goats leaping from peak to
peak in the Tyrol or the Andes who donate silky
hides to bike riders whizzing by the University
of Washington and old ladies trudging
on swollen feet along the trail. Imagine
sure-footed goats ending between the legs
of elite cyclists with skin-tight bodies:
what better terminus for a goat
than to nestle testicles
at high speed?
Though the Mysteries
are secret,
the Great God Pan
may yet be satisfied.

PAPAL TOMBS, BASILICA OF ST. PETER

The electronic voice—*This is a sacred place;*
maintain silence and reflection—repeated in six
languages ends the possibility of silence.
The river of hot tourists prompts reflection
on cool lunch: a glass of Frascati, a plate
of antipasti. In the dimness, devotees
kneel before popes who dine on heavenly
food: eucharistic bread, ambrosia, divinity.
My eye falls on yet another label for yet
another bronzed and marbled tomb. Here
lies Charles Edward Stuart—Hey!
I read the dates. It's Bonnie Prince Charlie!
I am startled awake. How can this be?
His bones, a stone's throw from Peter's own,
lie banished, on alien soil, the end of the line:
six feet of holy ground in exchange for a nation.
I want to pat the brazen crown in sympathy.
Instead I snake through the crowd, ushered
into the light by a voice in six languages:
Exit left. When you leave, there is no return.

RANUCCIO TOMASSONI

run through by Caravaggio
in 1606 in a fight over a girl—
Fillide Melandroni—his model
Saint Catherine, his Virgin Mary,
his Judith beheading Holofernes
with a bloody sword—the sword
in the painting modeled on
the same sword he used
to run through that pimp,
Ranuccio Tomassoni. Caravaggio's
paint-covered hands are bloody;
he flees from the churches of Rome
to the churches of Naples,
a celebrity painter and brawler-in-taverns,
where he murders twice again
until his patrons can do no more
to save him. Naked as a penniless
apprentice he creeps back to Rome
for pardon, but dies of fever in Grosetto,
his body never found. Ranuccio
Tomassoni is four years dead:
they molder together in Tuscan ground,
the alabaster skin and black eyebrows
of their battlefield—Fillide Melandroni—
alive on canvas, forever young.

TACOMA SCREW

It's not what you think. It's just an industrial
fabricator in Washington State: tools, pipe fittings,
screws. You, however, thought of bad
behavior, something performed in brothels,
the Wild West. Or perhaps you thought
it was the moniker of someone bad and dashing:
Don Giovanni, Mack the Knife, Tacoma Screw.
I don't blame you.
It's the nature of double entendres—
everybody's smutty joke.
                    Maybe the old gent
back in 1892, hanging his shingle, setting out stores,
came up with a little pun for the loggers
on the corduroy road. Not the sort of codger
to mind that cyclists a century later
ride by and snigger at the innocent past—
Tacoma Screw!—as though
the risqué is invented anew in the mind
of every kid on a mountain bike.
                    On the other hand
there could have been a Tacoma Screw,
like Butch Cassidy or Billy the Kid—
seductive as Casanova,
glamorous as Zorro,
renowned among mountain men and dancing girls
in rotgut saloons all up and down the Columbia,
famous for his threaded weapon—
once sunk, so hard to remove.

LA BOHÈME

After the overture, before the curtain rises on the garrets
of Paree, the conductor turns to the audience
and points his baton at me: You be Mimi, he says.
We need a real woman, as common as olives—
it's what Puccini wanted!
        My velvet seat ejects.
I land backstage at the director's feet. He dresses me
in chintz and a shawl, gives me a list of cues.
What? I say, No lines, no songs?
Make it up as you go along,
he says, it's more real that way.
        I'm thrilled! I pounce on stage—
a big grin on my face. I sashay up and down,
missing every cue. I wave at Mom and Dad
and all my friends. I say things like
Golly! Cafe Momus! and Oh! Vino! Grat-zee-ay!
At the end I tell Rudolfo: Really, I feel fine.
I take a bow.
        Backstage, the Director looks
grim. I realize what a fool I've been and apologize—
I'm so chagrined. *Ce n'est rien,* he says,
taking back the costume and pointing to the door.
You ordinary Mimis are who we do this for.

THE FUR-FACED BOYS

Watching Spanish TV—
(I don't know Spanish)
I see a Mexican family
sitting on their bed together
talking to a balding, excitable reporter.
The females—mom and ribboned baby—look normal,
and daddy seems like any rough, good natured
peasant in past or present history. But their three boys,
infant, child and adolescent, look out from faces
coated with fur like cats, or dogs with quiet, candid eyes.
I think I understand the conversation
from occasional words, and the mother's tone
to the fat, balding man:
        Normale in otro ways?
Ah, si, they go to school and make good grades.
        And their friends? *Los niños* can be so *malitos*!
Si, but they are used to this by now. The doctors say
no hay medicina, and we have *no dinero* anyhow.
Mira: but see how the hair curls down their cheeks in tender waves?
Overlook the way they ought to be—you can see the beauty,
like the faces of your beloved animals: the cat you sleep with,
the dog so smart it saved your life, your plow horse.
These are noble creatures, and this fur,
it brings attention to the eyes—the brightness, full of life,
the good simplicity of beasts. *Mihos*:
be like your animal relations: be glad
you stand apart from the naked race of men.

GIRL

I saw a girl of six or so, twirling
her stuffed bunny by the ear
sauntering after her parents
on the Burke Gilman Trail.
It put me in mind, as I passed on my bike,
of Rosie, a puppy stuffed with nylons,
given at my baptism decades and decades ago.
Though proffered bears and kittens,
lambkins and dollies, I chose to chew
on Rosie's paws, spit up on her
stitched-on smile. I threw her
from my crib, the window,
the grocery cart, the high chair,
my Dad's old DeSoto—my mother
the faithful retriever. I flung Rosie
at siblings, neighborhood dogs,
the mailman, the milkman—at the night.
She escaped from shark-infested
linoleum, policed the toy-box prison,
rode with Annie Oakley, Roy Rogers,
the Cisco Kid, did everything
they did, and better—
just like that bunny, whirled like a lariat
in the Seattle sun by a swaggering
young girl on the Burke Gilman trail.

ATHENA IN SEATTLE

Along the lip of the blue Mediterranean
widows wear black from head to toe.
One always knows what to give Nonna
on her saint's day: another black
sweater, a black mantilla.
Back in Seattle, an old
woman on the Burke-Gilman Trail
wears all black but for her gray hair.
She seems to have been deposited
there as suddenly as Aphrodite left Helen
blinking and bewildered at Paris' feet
on Mount Ida. Some loving relative
has given her hiking sticks—black,
of course—which she carries like candles,
high before her as though to light
her way through the New World.
She shuffles along on the wrong
side of the trail, parting pélotons
of bikers as they charge toward her,
like Moses before a Red Sea
of beautiful boys in helmets. Or,
not to mix metaphors: she stands,
wands aloft, like Athena scattering
Achaeans as their armies rush before her.

LINES COMPOSED IN LINE

The unemployment waiting hall
is grid-like—red tiles beat time
along the floor matched by fluorescent
squares overhead that create
a vanishing point neat as Leonardo's,
while we jobless form a fresco worthy
of the Quattrocento: God's perfect order
aligned in perspective like DaVinci's
Last Supper—sightlines knotted
behind Christ's head.
Disciples turn from their betrayals
and their bread to see, see nothing
but his face—the lines insist.
Sacred lines, even here—
bearded prophets wait
no place to rest their heads beside
madonnas in their jeans:
the lines insist.

ON READING YEATS' "LEDA AND THE SWAN"

Only a man would ask if Leda got,
bill-bruised and thrust
by a protean god,
wisdom
before she dropped.
Only a man would
use the word
caress
for death-on-wing,
deploy his penetrating
rhyme to honor
feathered glory.
Unlike a man, unblinded
by the splendor of a god-crime
I can ask:
How does a human woman
hatch two eggs?
Front-to-front or
doggy-style that laying on?
What honking shriek means
Fuck me, bitch
in swan?

HERA AT THE PIANO

She of the white arms
playing her eternal music
of domesticity and calm
yet when infidelity
storms the keys her music
murders Semele
and all those girls
whose only flaw
was to draw the eye
of fertility
to their white bosoms
her posture is forever
perfect her arms
the divine continuum
of passion:
love to rage

REPORT TO NEW YORK
Dateline: Burke Gilman Trail

I used to enter Central Park from Columbus,
walking the lower loop a few times before dinner
when the city was leaving work and working out
together. Half the fun was looking at each other
in training gear and gauging our youth
against another's age. I remember
the old woman in yellow, folded over—
staring down at her white sneakers—
who never missed a day.
But now I ride a bike in Seattle, slowly:
a turtle on the road as boys in yellow jerseys
and red helmets pass me in wakes of air
that wobble my bike toward the brambles.
The trail—cut into the side of a steep hill—
has houses perched atop and strung along
the banks of Lake Washington below. A railroad
ran here once, hauling clear-cut logs to the ports
of Puget Sound. Now it drains Seattle into suburbs,
both directions: Lake Forest, Shoreline, Redmond,
Olympic Hills, Fremont, Ballard. Citizens here
don't want a Central Park—too communal.
They're descendants of Yukon miners
and mountain men, of Swedish loggers
and eccentrics forced West. They need to be
alone in public, surrounded
by natural wonders:
Mount Rainier beyond the lake—
as solitary as we who ride or walk
in single file
up and down the trail.

TWO RACCOONS

Big as small gondolas, they glide
low to the ground, their masks
like Venetians at *Carnivale*,
their ringtails a witty disguise—
aristocrats hushing across my lawn
to the party where we *hoi polloi*
are not invited. I ogle them
from the porch, imagining
the bright palace where they dance
all night in their high-heeled feet
on the bones of squirrels, cats,
possums. How easy to forget
they're wild—rather they seem
superior in their elegant command
of evening. In the morning
one raccoon may lie on the side
of the road, tail askew,
as though dead from despair
that celerity has replaced
the slow luxury of celebration.

THOSE KILLED BY SERPENTS

Ravisius Textor, Doctor of Rhetoric (1480-1524), assigns a theme.

Write your composition, boys,
on one of the ancients here compiled
and the manner of his dying.
This is the list of those who were suicides,
and those who were parricides.
(Yes, boys, they killed their fathers.)
Here is the list of drowned persons
and those who have given their names to bodies of water
by having been drowned in them.
Here is the list of those killed or dismembered by horses,
or killed by the fall of horses.
These are those killed by serpents,
(so are we all, boys, all killed by the serpent
who tempted Eve).You may write about
those killed by boars, those killed by lions,
those killed by dogs, and those killed by various beasts.
Here too is the list of individuals
struck by lightning,
individuals dead by hanging,
and those dead by crucifixion.
(Our Lord was one of many, boys,
but the only one who rose again.)
And here are those dead by thirst
or hunger, as well as those consumed
by fire. You will also find here persons
cast off precipices,
dead from falling staircases,
and people swallowed up by the earth.

**

(Hell took them, boys,
though the ancients were not subject
to the full justice of Heaven.)
And here are the victims of sudden death.
and those done away by poison,
by the machinations of wizards,
of husbands, of wives, of siblings,
and thwarted children. (Sin instructs, my boys,
as well as virtue). And finally,
lest you be discouraged,
here is the list of death by pleasure:
those who died of food and drink,
those who died from laughter
and those, my boys, who died from joy.

THE TRAVELERS

They appeared on the brink of Judea, like the pluck
of a tuning string: Gatháspa, Melchias, Pudizar,
their shared language astronomy (unscrolling their charts,
gesticulating at the sky). It wasn't luck
that brought them together in the desert,
but the quality of their separate magic.
Truth to tell, the ushering star
was combined with the old constellations,
and when wind whipped clouds through the chilly night,
they couldn't see anything very well.
Until they found each other they had begun to doubt
they would find anyone, much less a monarch
nobody knew about.
But now they were three: a Babylonian mage,
a Persian seer, and from the land of Ind
a wizard who could derive gold from the ores of Malabar.
Now they had their triple art to take them
toward the thing they sought: a Hebrew king
in the nest of Rome.

Then imagine their alarm
when they found the king a newborn
in a lean-to of date fronds and olive branches.
How quickly they erected an incense altar
to ward off the seven evil demons!
How they sang incantations, wove spells against Pazuzu
who brings contagion, and Lamashtu
who poisons breast milk. They tried to explain,
through clouds of myrrh and cinnamon,
which rites the baffled parents should perform.
But the girl and her old spouse seemed as innocent of danger

as the infant son, or the sheep and mules
they sat among. Gatháspa pressed an amulet of gold
into the father's fist: *Keep it no matter what*
he insisted in his tongue *so that Namtaru*
will not take him to the underworld!
They left the parents plenty of resins, oils,
and frankincense to burn, though doubted
they'd comply with instructions.
Each magus thought sadly, turning back to the East:
This poor little king will die.
May the gods hide his name from the evil ones.

ON THE TARMAC AT INDIANAPOLIS

There's a storm in Chicago—plane won't fly.
Nature's a-churning: white out, sleet, rain, snow.
Above the clouds—somewhere—is clear blue sky.

I'm buckled in. I have my ham-on-rye,
my crossword, caffé latte, H_2O.
But—the storm's in Chicago. Plane won't fly.

Glum silence, then a baby starts to cry.
Watches tick—flight connections fade, then go.
Yet somewhere, above the clouds, is clear blue sky.

Worry-warts pray, cynics gripe, others try
to sleep or read a book because they know
there's a storm in Chicago—plane won't fly.

My iPod has two thousand songs, but I
don't want Johnny Cash or Rigoletto.
I want the clouds to clear. I want blue sky.

Rascal Vicissitude! You send the fly
in the soup and the storm to Chicago,
ephemeral as a cloud. Plane won't fly
for now, but sometime—oh, soon!—clear blue sky.

THIS GOLDEN LESSON

This golden lesson short and plain
    Gives not the mind nor memory pain
And every conscience must approve
    The universal law of love.

—Isaac Watts, Hymn XXXVIII

SPECKLED EGG

I want to write a poem about a speckled egg
because the assonating "eh" sounds
go so well together. Even better, I can use
"freckle" and "shell," then work in a bird
of some kind. I might find a metaphor
for the fragile beauty of a speckled egg:
its pattern a microcosmic galaxy
coating the dome of heaven. Then,
reflecting on the life inside, I might observe
the emerging bird peck-peck-pecking—
then exploding through its shell
like the Big Bang!
I can't recall why I wanted this artifact,
or who gave it to me in the first place.
It sits with all the other gifts
a poet receives: pressed flowers,
twigs of colored berries, crystals, oddly shaped
pebbles, tiny bones. Something twangs
the soul and says *hatch me*
if you have incubation time
and don't press down too hard.
Even so, I might mourn the bird
that was never born for the sake
of my reflections.

THE MAN WHO WANTS YOU

The man who wants you
is never in the place
you are. He is in Brooklyn,
you are in Chicago;
he is painting houses,
you work for Microsoft;
he is into bowling and computer games;
you love stargazing
and poetry.

The man who wants you
is never in the time
you are: he is twenty years older,
rugged, romantic, teaching
Shakespeare or biology;
you are a coed with big eyes
in the back row of desire.
Or years later, the man who wants you
sits in the front row of your classroom
raising his hand, hanging on your
every word, trailing you to your office
with a thousand eager comments;
you are old enough to be his mother,
the last crush of his childhood

The man who wants you
missed all of his cues, never
knew you were the One
until he had a wife and a house
full of responsibilities;
with the clarity of hindsight

he tracks down your number,
calls you past midnight
to weep and imagine
your phantom marriage.
The man who wants you
is never where you are — you
with your laundry basket
and your five-year-old car.
The man who wants you
is in Tahiti or Shangri-La —
the moon, the lagoon,
the gardenia on the nightstand.

UNREASONABLE WOMAN

Sometimes, alone at home, I say into the air
"Bastard! Thieves!" or sometimes,
"I love you" to nobody, in order to hear
my voice, and to address the people
who ought to have been here, fighting
with me, whom I could resent for hemming
me in so that I could never have
this solitude. For not loving me enough,
or not appreciating my feelings.
"I love you" I say to the one
who did not believe me, who never came here,
that thief, who let my hair grow gray
without him, that bastard.

I DREAMED OF MY MOTHER'S CLOTHES

I dreamed of my mother's clothes:
opened an antique wardrobe—all her
clothes were there that I remember,
from crinolines to hose

with elegant seams
up the back; her housecoat,
her scarves that float
in perfume; I seem

to stand before a bank
of fabric memory,
my mother with me—
casual or swank

in gown, blouse, and slack—
as I rummage through
saying "Oh! I remember you,
and you!"—the fecund rack

giving me my mother
back again, and me a child
in her warm closet, clothes piled
around me like other

arms, the camphor scent of caring.
I find a green remnant
of the tweed coat she sent
me away to college in—faring

**

alone—long before she left herself,
an old lady in tidy gym
clothes, eyes rheumy, brain dim,
leaving spangled shawls on a back shelf.

In the dream I clutch the fiber
body of her, the outermost skin—
embrace it all, remember when
the clothes, and I, were filled by her.

YESHUA SUMMONED THE TWELVE

and gave them the skill
to drive out demons by a word. He taught them
to cure every ill they came across—
palsy, dog bite, leprosy,
even horse fever and diseases of evil pleasure:
pox and the bloody rectum—
ills the rest of the rabbis claimed were
God's measure of wrath against Sodom
and Gomorrah.

But Peter argued with the Rabbi:
Best and worst get equal cures?
He spit in the coals: *Not from me.*
He peered at the brethren—
The cost of unnatural sin is death!
Peter planted his scaly hands on his thighs:
What kind of rabbi do you want me to be?
His boast floated over the brethren. They nodded:
there's no cure for some things.

But the Rabbi took Peter in his arms,
the way a mother will take up her simple child,
or a man his lover: *I forgive you*
he murmured, as if Peter's mind
was on wielding his cock in the shadows,
crowing over boys and bad women.

Yeshua kissed Peter's stricken, guilty face:
Make them all well, he said,
for your own sake.

SAN XAVIER DEL BAC

You drive miles into the desert
to find a jewel glittering
in the sand. O how every surface
is encrusted with shells, cherubs—
four centuries of prayers!
How the old saint himself
lies swaddled in gold, working
milagros in the modern
world. One of many wonders occurred
right here, contractors and sun-baked
laborers returning this crude treasure
to glory, and the wide-eyed saints
stand amazed to find themselves
resurrected and restored.

VISTA POINT

I rode a bike to San Francisco Bay
where a pelican soared alone
over Vista Point. There were neither
boats nor tourists. No ferries
nor sails nor other signs of life.
Only this pelican and I,
alone together.
            Except for kelp. Wands
of soft green kelp
under yellowy water,
and the grey pelican
flapping its leathery wings,
in an aqua sky, he and I
alone together.
            Except for kelp and one silvery
jacksmelt in that big brown beak,
we three—bird, fish, person—
(and the kelp) alone together.
            Except for floating plankton,
in their millions, leopard sharks,
and halibut, shiners, crabs
and jacksmelt filling the bay.
And of course, the purple shade
I stood in, of acacias, hibiscus, and great
deodar cedars, home to Bewick's
wren, hummingbirds, Cooper's
hawks, and California towhees,
all of us alone together
at Vista Point.

HELIUM BALLOONS

They are the size of a human head,
supposing it red, purple, or Mylar,
"Happy Birthday!" glittering across the face.
In a car, however, helium balloons
are a passel of nosy aunts. Each one bobs
toward you on a scrawny ribbon neck,
blocks your rearview mirror, your windows,
intrudes on your business with delicate nods,
floats ever closer (with sad little bows)
to the steering wheel, as though it is not
your fault you are late, that you tailgate,
that you cannot find the parking lot.
Not your fault you are last to arrive
at the restaurant, the moment of surprise
missed, your gift and your fist of balloons
an afterthought, the Mylar aunts as irrelevant,
though kindly met, as they (sighing)
have learned to expect.

STROLLING THE FRONT AT LARGS

A place out of novels—the kind where
seaside towns form a peaceful scrim
for the tumult in the heroes' breasts.
Our breasts are calm.
        We stroll the esplanade, capture furtive
        sun in company with skipping children,
        parents pale, elders with ancient
        terriers barking deafly at sailing gulls.
        Fish and chips at The Green Shutters,
        a walk with ice cream and 99s, we lick
        our knuckles, saying little.
Eighteen holes on the putting green,
my recalcitrant ball on a stroll
of its own. You block its wayward
trips with your shoe, congratulate
my lucky shots. We fudge our way
to a comfortable tie.
        On a bench fronting the sea we sit
        for an hour. Boys throw rocks at gulls,
        skip stones over the Clyde. Babies
        cry in prams. Girls whisper together,
        ignore the sky for boys. Lovers
        walk by in slow embrace. Silently
        we compose poems in our heads.
How calm we are; quiet as an hourglass,
as though eternal, like the river at our feet
and the still, inflated clouds, the green
hills of the Hebrides along the front at Largs.

AT THE FOOT OF THE GREAT TABLE

It's a long, long table,
so long I can't see
the head of it—
only the candles, the flowers,
the tinkling crystal,
like little bells of longing.
I am only the governess
in a great family,
eating below the salt
with the children:
me and my poverty
and my wonderful mind.

LIPSTICK

When I'm old, and my breasts
hang against my chest
like empty pockets;
when my irises have turned milky,
and the creases in my face
look like a drawstring bag—
then I'll wear the reddest lipstick
I can get, the scarlet kind you
find at Woolworth's for 99 cents.
I'll be one of those old ladies
whose smeary red lips stand like a tent-pole
in the middle of my face,
holding up the center no matter how
the rest flags in folds around.
I will fly this red banner as if to say:
Look at me! You, too, will die
by the inch
from the outside in:
but if you ever had a night with a man
who really, really likes women,
your memories live in the lips!
They grin long past the time
your joints could hold them up.
These memories live in the mouth,
the old, red mouth,
just like that young one,
just like that hidden one,
when the body was glorious!

FOR VALENTINE'S DAY

I nearly bought you a parakeet for the way
he hid his orange beak under a blue wing,
slept in perfect peace—motionless—
like you sleep.
        But then I thought I ought to ask
permission to give you a creature
so like my feelings for you:
alive and lovely, prehensile feet
on a solid perch: so much care required
(if not cuttlebones and birdfeed
then at least to play, conversation).
        We might call him Blue Cupid,
both of us whistling to him, chirping
in the green light that filters
through the ficus in your window.
Each day we could free him from his cage
—could risk his flying away
because he would be happy.
        But I left him dozing
on his perch at Petco knowing
that parakeets—like doves and robins,
eagles and falcons—are everywhere,
that they carry all we need in beak
and talon: dreams and earthworms,
olive branches, arrows, and satin ribbons
inscribed with hearts: *Amor vincit omnia*.

MARRIAGE AT CANA

The miracle is that anyone can love,
look eye-to-eye without turning away.
That youth exchanges urgency for order:
man with his bristling arrows, woman
with her reservoir of life. Seasons die
and revive: husband, wife,
husband, wife.

Yeshua is young himself. He wants to
stamp his feet, slap his thighs,
sing at this wedding! He wants to
look at girls whose toes have
tiny silver bands, whose veils have
little trilling bells. He wants to
flick his fingers and ring
the little bells. He wants to
braid and tangle, run, pursue —
there is no verb for all he wants to do!
He says *Yes!* to everything: skewered goat,
wedding bread, and to his mother
pressing him for wine. Why should he subdue
his gift within the logos of his mind?
Yeshua gives the wedding guests the best wine ever made:
he may as well. Even though it's not his time, the end,
he knows, is swelling on the vine.

**

53

Only the sober steward stands transfixed
by water, deepening into scarlet,
spiraling through the amphorae. He tastes it:
By the staff of Moses! he cries.
What time destroys it cannot uncreate:
the bridegroom sits beside his happy bride,
worlds on the brink. Yeshua sings,
dances, drinks, commits: he feels as though
he's wedded everything.

ROSENKAVALIER

Octavian rolls out of bed
with the Field Marshal's wife.
She is elegant, experienced—
the Marschallin!
Engel! he cries, *Du! Du! Du!*
What more can he say,
being so young, but
Angel! and You! You! You!

But we, being so old,
recover in bed
discussing *As You Like It*
and the nuances of jokes
we heard at a dinner party.
We comment on each other's
growing stomachs,
aching shoulders.
We pat each other's
rumpled pillows, sip water,
put our PJs back on.

Nevertheless, sweetheart,
Du! Du! Du!

FELLOW-CLAY

Great God I own thy sentence just,
And nature must decay
I yield my body to the dust
to dwell with fellow-clay.

—Isaac Watts, Hymn VI

LUCIDITY

Language must thicken
like scabs over wounds;
to obscure the raw flesh
under that fascinating crust
we love to pick at.
Pestering clarity!
Who can trust an image
or a metaphor, clear
as trees and water?

I want to tattoo my words
with the ballpoint of my pen,
to Queequeg plain English
with fantastic designs,
I want to make you hack
through an underbrush
of verbiage, or chip at its solidity
with the pick axe of your mind.

Yet all my veils are transparent,
and my designs like ivy on a monument:
Beneath the form and filigree I weave,
you know there is an angel
or an obelisk underneath.

RUNAWAY

By the time his parents missed him
the night was at its prime: a moon so white and full
they hadn't lit their lanterns on the way back to Nazareth.
See them panic and hurry back to Jerusalem!
Search inns and stables until morning,
push through leaves of pomegranate trees calling *Shua! Shua!*
hoping their son was asleep in the hot shade.
For three days they searched the streets, through herds
of goats and sheep, scattered sheaves in the fields,
combed through beards of hemp drying on the red clay walls.
See them approach the temple
ready to sell their ox to make burnt offering for their child.
They pause, afraid to go in, as if to tell the rabbis
was to forsake their offspring.
Let's search some more, she begged.
But Yusef set his face and went forward.
They spotted Yeshua tucked among the cluster of rabbis.
She knew that look: dazed, head cocked to the right.
Listening to the olives grow, his parents said when he got that way.
And this was like him, too: no defense —
just amazement, as if all boys ran away
to engage in the *hence* and *wherefore*
of rabbinical debate.
Nothing they said would shame him;
not his father's anger nor his mother's tears.
Don't do it again! all the way back to Nazareth.
See Shua roll his eyes and sigh. He says *I won't,*
telling his parents the time-worn, necessary lie.

THE LANGUAGE LACKS A NECESSARY SLANT

The language lacks a necessary slant
for honoring a claim of family sorrow:
there ought to be a word for "grieving aunt"

as wives' bereavement—no more permanent
or complete—is recognized by *widow*.
But language lacks a necessary slant

describing that same isolated want
for her whose only child was a nephew.
There ought to be a word for "grieving aunt"

as *orphan* is the word for infant
severed from its mother: something empty, hollow.
The language lacks a necessary slant

describing barren hours, days absent
of hope, the flat, attenuated view.
There ought to be a word for a grieving aunt

who had that younger life, now sent
through time to age alone. My only Andrew,
the language lacks a necessary slant:
there isn't any word for "grieving aunt."

ON SEEING KEATS' DEATHROOM

Mortality is gathering
in my inability to sleep, the way a flight of stairs
looms up too steep for my knees.
I could almost be your mother
you were so young when you came here to die.
When I was a girl, a hundred and fifty years after you,
I stared at the Roman sky.
I sat on the Spanish Steps and gazed at your window
weeping, in the way of girls, over death and poetry.
Why did I grow up to write poems
that can't keep the lamps of Arcady alight?
When I think of your tubercular eye,
glittering up at these painted rafters,
(how sick you must have been of those blue flowers!)
your teeming brain no refuge
from the feud between time and desire,
I know that the pain of modest talent
is rude compared to a great gift sinking
beneath the main of necessity:
your light, the consequences of love,
that magnitude of vision: gone, my refractor,
gone from this room where I sit, and from the world.
        My feet hurt. I sit at your secretary shifting
through ephemera: letters, a deathbed sketch.
Soon I'll buy souvenirs, return
to the glare of sun and marble.

THE KILLING SPEED

We grew so fast our bones hurt
when we were five. Remember how
the cuts grew over? They disappeared
like paths disappearing
in a jungle. It pushed us out,
that healing speed—out of our jeans!
Our ankles dangled from the cuffs,
our buttons flew away like crying
birds. We pounded on ourselves
with jungle gyms, tore off hunks of skin
on broken bark. Dogs bit us with their alligator
teeth, and still our cells
divided—pulled themselves apart
to heal the gaps our playing made.

They taught, when I was still in school,
that atoms are like universes:
sun-like nuclei enlooped by planet-particles.
And as we orbit neatly through the void,
so cells divide, repeating paths of order.

Experience has taught me better.
Splitting cells can lose control—
fling themselves apart like creatures
in the wild run amok. And if you're five,
as Andrew was, what stitched the cuts
together so fast you grew overnight
like a jungle vine, grabs you fast,
like a galloping lion, kills you
with the speed of light.

IRISES AND TULIPS

Irises seem particularly
dead when they die:
their stems still so green
yet heads withered and
drained of color
like old women who have
forgotten where they live
and the names of their
children.

Tulips die extravagantly:
shed petals like strippers
in a bar of applauding men,
stems yellow and brown,
all used up. They seem
to die happily, as if
death were a lifelong
commitment.

SONNET

I don't care if loveliness is spreading
its delicate array against the sky
in feathered colors. Let flowers do their budding
on their own. They don't need me or my
attention for their gentle business,
or know if I drag by them all alone.
I don't want birds to puff their summer softness,
shedding darling shakes of evening rain
that make you long to hold them to your cheek.
The sunlight—too incongruous a burden—
bears down my sagging shoulders like a thief
in reverse. I don't accept these things so soaring,
bright and fragrant relishing the sun
in leaping velvet green with Andrew gone.

FINAL DIET

How much
does a boy weigh
when he's five?
Thirty pounds?
Thirty-five or more?
I am thirty pounds above
my trim. I've gained and lost
and gained and lost
the likes of him.
Now he's gone
and I can't gain him back.
I hunker in my overcoat
of fat, collecting
underneath my skin
the flesh that can't replace
the living thing,
and think of dying:
dying makes us thin.

SCHUBERTIAD

"...what may have impelled some observers of Schubert's behavior to speak of abominations and vile practices was the prospect of sexual relations between a man and a youth, with its connotations of child molestation and its glimpse of a taboo realm of experience."
> —Maynard Solomon
> *"Franz Schubert and the Peacocks of Benvenuto Cellini"*

Though the brain splits
like a walnut
between ecstasies,
all is one
in the cadenza:
music born
on the instrument
he played on,
beating out measures
between the legs;
breaking in tender bodies
like a new violin,
syphilis the rosin
on his bow.
Where elegance is not
restraint,
where purity of form
is unchaste,
we who soar participate
in the knowledge
of who paid
for our pleasures.

**

What became of those
children, offered up
in rising cadences
on the lap of the Maestro?

WASTED TIME

And now I look at television,
smoke a cigarette, think of who to call
on Monday, what to have for dinner.
My nephew's picture by the brawling tube
is silent while the bedlam carries on.
His two-year-old, pre-illness self
preserved inside the frame: his frown
is for his mother, who arrested him mid-
adventure, to take the last shot
on a roll of film—her boy, on his trike,
by the kitchen door. Cancer won't enter
the picture for six months, death
for three years more. He leans forward
on the handlebars, impatient for his future.
My sister lets him go, winds his exposures
into a little cylinder. I leave my share
of him there, with his mother taking pictures
by their kitchen door.
                              And now I switch
the channels, rumple through the weekend *Times*,
brush crumbcake off the sheets. I shift
my weight. What a string of hours rolls by,
a long, long string. We tried, we tried.
We tried to fix him here.

BEFORE

Walk nude through the house,
lifting a breast with each hand,
feeling each liquid weight shift
as you walk; feeling,
as you hold them up,
that you are young again,
that they are at once your children
and yourself; knowing
that these companions rise and fall
in solidarity with you; that you
may have to give them up
one by one
to save yourself;
that they will be sacrificed,
these flowing solids,
these kissing stations,
these secret reservoirs,
for you; knowing
that you will keen for them
as for lost children, feel the guilty
weight of blood money.
Walk naked through the house,
hold them now, as you might cherish
your old parents,
your memories of youth:
ask forgiveness, be reconciled,
before they go.

THE ARITHMETIC OF MOURNING

Forty birthdays died with you,
two graduations, forty Christmas days:
I may live for forty years or more,
but now, because you died before me, boy,
I stare ahead at all those gifts
not given, bounty filling up my empty hands.

I am a childless mother, who hands
that weight of love to siblings' children: you,
your cousin, sister, brother, are the gifts
my siblings gave me; and for those family days
of celebration I have planned your presents months ahead. Boy,
you have deprived me: you won't take my presents anymore.

And I—I can't enjoy your presence anymore,
your goofy little humor. You danced, hands
and arms flapping, knees churning the carpet—a boy-
galliard of overflowing spirits. We called you
Crazy Legs Simpson; just like a rascal; your days
filled up with silly songs and all those childish gifts.

I calculate about two hundred gifts
I didn't get to give you. What more
concrete burden than the gifts of all your birthdays,
shirts and sweaters, games, circus trips—hands
sticky with cotton candy; planning pleasures for you
that were, certainly, my own joy. Oh little boy,
Thank God you can't be here to see the grief one boy
can cause by his going. I can't stop buying gifts

**

71

for you. They pile up, the puzzles, the stickers you
collected for your album, the banana harmonica, more
kiddie books, more records; a Kermit watch with froggie hands
to point the hours you will never count, the lost days.
I wonder, if I'd known you had so few days,
would I have multiplied my giving? Heaping a boy
with thirty presents every Christmas, filling his hands
with accelerating gifts, teen-age gifts?
I picture myself mounding you with suits and ties, more
to bind you here: a briefcase, a savings bond, a basketball. You

left my days, my holidays diminished, my gifts like trash without a boy
to take them. More good things load these hands to sinking without you.

LAYING FLOWERS ON A GRAVE AT LARGS

for Brian Whittingham

Should the dead have such a view?
he asks, standng at his brother's grave
on a ridge above the Firth of Clyde,
blue like another sky below us,
green mountains ranged around.
The dour rain had burned away.
Michelangelo clouds
touched fingers above our heads
and distant sea.

Half his brother's stone is blank, patient.
We lay carnations—two pinks, two hearts,
two clouds—that will fade like the boy
he knew better than he can tell.
The view is picnic-pretty, displayed
to make the heart glad. I imagine
fowk and bairns gathered round
a paisley cloth, baps, scones,
and flasks of tea.

Aye, old friend, it's well deserved,
this view, a legacy for you and yours
for aye an' aye. Where ever he is,
we join him soon enough. So place your
own remains where those you love
see clouds remake themselves no end
above the Firth of Clyde
and distant sea.

PANTOUM ON THE TENTH ANNIVERSARY
OF ANDREW'S DEATH

A little Chinese girl pushes a yellow bunny in a pink pram
down Court Street. Something in her childish pride
reminds me of you, who would have been
taller than I am now, but were smaller than she when you died.

Down Court Street, something in her childish pride
makes me look at tall boys, about fifteen,
taller than I am now. Smaller than she when you died,
I try to imagine your five-year-old face as a teen.

I look for tall boys about fifteen
with blondish hair and farcical wit.
I try to imagine your five-year-old face as a teen
and the comedian living behind it.

Tall, gangling boys acting silly in public
remind me of you, who would have been,
at this age, both treasure and pain in the neck.
Oh, sad little Chinese girl, pushing your yellow bunny in a pink pram!

THE DEATH OF THOMAS MERTON

Remember Thomas Merton who died in Thailand?
His monk's habit laid aside, he showered in the skin of Adam.

Wet as a newborn baby, he stood in pooled water and touched
an electric fan.
The current flowed from his outstretched hand to the blessed earth
beneath his feet.

He lay blackened by molecules that crossed the path of his heart.
How electricity enters the body like a soul, seeking a better place.

He was transformed by the current, converted yet again
from the alpha of baptism to the omega of Siloe, the pool of silence.

His conversion shocked the Pope and the Dalai Lama.
Dorothy Day and Father Berrigan were shocked;
Nelson Mandela in his prison and Ceasar Chavez in his field
were shocked.

Stunned were the Quakers in their meetings and Catholic Workers
in their slums,
monks in their zendos, monks in their stalls were stunned.

The spirit of God broods upon the waters of creation.
First comes the water, then the shock of light.

Who was Thomas Merton?
Ready and naked in a bathroom in Thailand?
born cleanly by molecules into a better place?

**

How the arc of life is a knotted line,
tangles twisted into the hum of language,

How a young man, entangled, sought the path of silence,
yet the tangle of writing was required of him.

He wrote: *I seek to speak to you, in some way, as your own self.*
Who can tell what this may mean?

I myself do not know,
but if you listen, things will be said that are perhaps not written in this book.
And this will be due not to me but to the One who lives and speaks in both.

That One called him to the Abbey of Gesthemane.
That One called him to a shower in Thailand.

Dressed as Adam, his outstretched hand touched the hand of God.
First comes the water, then the shock of light.

KYRIE PANTOKRATOR

The world was not for me, but for my brothers,
the horses, the science kits, the classrooms,
the rough training for the world, which was not
for me, but for my husbands, the work, the money,
the camaraderie over drinks and waitresses, which
was not for me but for my fathers, the wives, the tidy
homes and waiting children, the warm bed,
which was not for me.
        I beat the chest of my soul.

The clear path was not for me but for the scions,
the boys of promise and grace, their football fields,
the locker room and all its promises, which was not
for me but for the scholars, their tutors, the books
and allowances, the mighty potential, which
was not for me but for the junior partners,
their swaddles of opportunity, the slap on the back,
which was not for me.
        I bite the tongue of my mind.

The audience was not for me but for the speakers,
their podiums and printing presses, the bull horns which
were not for me but for the soldiers, their flags and taxes,
the guns and petroleum, their certainty of righteousness
which was not for me but for the kings, the popes, the presidents,
their parades and treasure, their chest of ribbons,
which was not for me.
        I brandish the fist of my bowels.

**

The Church was not for me but for the Adams,
the ones who look like You in their secret bodies,
like the Father and the suffering Son in his ribs
and rags, which were not for me but for the saints,
their faith and miracles. Only the martyrs,
their persecutions, their resistance, the hopes
of forgiveness for their jealousy, their cowardice,
their despair, Pantokrator, are for me.
      I bend the knee of my heart.

MONK'S GATE

The abbey is no more, its gate
of sturdy birchwood merely a traffic circle,
the commemorative stone arch blackened
by honking fumes. From the abbey
over fields of timothy grass
they likely passed, to the basilica—
a brown line with capuchins
of mottled white—to form
a landscape of prayer against
the landscape of larch and maple.
Monk's Gate, the basilica's side door,
faces the ghostly abbey,
opens to monks no more.

Neither does the Shepherd's Gate admit
either shepherds or sheep, and the captains
of Captain's Gate are gone, with all
their arcane skills, to the murky past,
leaving traces of their passages on signs,
and doors, and wine labels, on quaint boards
swinging on chains over public houses:
"Friar's Gate"—the fat old fellow
tonsured, with a tankard in his fist.

Ubi sunt? Where are the widows
and cows who time out of mind
entered Widow's Gate and Cowsgate?
Monks and nuns, friars, chapmen,
yeomen and queens in such abundance

$**$

the gates still bear their names?
Gone, gone—exited this coil
along the broad way or the narrow,
flowing through gates that we
(in our boutiques and tanning salons)
disbelieve: the one of red-hot iron or—
Hallelujah!—the one
of shimmering pearl.

ANDREW'S BEAR ADDRESSES THE MOURNERS

We hold you in our fuzzy arms and paws,
we plush ducks and teddies, or
we blankets wrap you in beloved shreds. You gnaw

the fabric, suck your favorite finger or
hold your sex; we rock you to sleep
in your black crib. Your forget our succor

when you grow up, but we keep
your last appointment—we come back again
when your time is up. You need

us—your ragged, childhood friends—
in the final dark that scares you
at the heartless and disintegrating end.

Are you surprised to see us? You
forgot our button eyes, the face
you loved. We comforters escort you

through the blindness to another place
where you have eyes again. You mend
and grow. But if we have to take

your life too young, when you still depend
upon our clutching care, then—up we spring!
The way you always knew we were—grand

**

81

and gorgeous, golden haunch and wing
filling up your little room. You wrap
your arms around our cushioned necks; we fling
away black—you leap to the light on our mighty backs!

GET UP, LITTLE GIRL!

The parents are desperate—their minds are
shattered. They weep, wring their faces:
they have moved beyond love to hysteria.
The father can stand it no longer.
He finds the traveling rabbi who makes people
well, elbows into the crowd, tries to move the man
to pity, clutching the rabbi's legs:
>   *Mark our daughter with your sign! She's dying!*
The father crouches, shaken, his appeal dry bark.
Yeshua is taken by those with violent needs.
He says to the father whose cheeks are raked with gravel:
>   *I will come.*
The crowd follows. But a message comes.
>   *Don't bother the rabbi. She's dead.*
The father falls down, howling: after weeks of prayer
and the Healer so close! Better doom than irony.
But the rabbi perseveres.
Afterward, what happened proved something to everyone:
>   *She was never sick*, said some;
>   *The rabbi is Elijah*, said others.
This is what the girl said:
>   *A man who loved me said, Get up!*
Her parents asked what she meant
and the towns people asked what she meant
and after the rabbi died and when she was old,
people kept asking her:
>   *What do you mean?*
But she said nothing more, not to her dying day.

THE SEVENTH ANGEL

Let the seventh angel sound on high,
    Let shouts be heard thro' all the sky
Kings of the earth with glad accord
    Give up your kingdoms to the Lord.

—Isaac Watts, Hymn LXV

TIME'S EQUATOR

As the instability of sea
ignores imaginary grids—
(the equatorial belly-belt fitted over
its churning curves tossing its riders
to the elements) so the orderly line of time—
like nuns pacing a cloister,
slipping rosary beads one-by-one
through clean fingers—
is not the procession it seems
but mere invention roped
around cascading days spun
from the whirling earth.

A fiction: Young Keats
in his meager cup of time
crossed a century to die young,
while Old Linnaeus
picked over nomenclature
in a long, long life
within the green hedge
of a century.
Dates on gravestones
curious to picnic strollers
are as real as an illusionist's
white rabbit, hopping silently
among disappearing tombs.

PRAYER

Ignore, O Mystery, this thing You made.
It trembles me to think on You,
genderless, less than fluttering tissue,
not like me or any thing I know.
I fear to conjure You with prayer,
lest your mighty zero zero in on me—
What might you do?
Extract a whirlwind from my mind?
Impregnate my old age?
Burden me with prophecy
then strike me blind?
Hold me, O Mystery,
in your sidelong view.
Insofar as you are good,
be good to me too; or leave me
with the pebbles of consolation:
other people, things to do.
Ignore, O Mystery, this thing
You made. It trembles me
to ponder You.

ON GOING IN

O Lord my God, in thee do I put my trust.
Save me from them that pursue me and deliver me,
Lest they tear my soul like a lion.

I

The torment of voices:
When are you going
to get...
When are you going
to be...
Who will you pick who will
pick you
like a fruit coming into
juice waiting to squirt
and burst
at the first squeeze?
And the boys: their busy faces.
And the urgency of men and their
verbs: screw, suck, bang,
squeeze.
And the infinitive future: to bear,
to wash, to feed, to do—and do,
and do. How do the other girls
see Romance
where I see the alien hair
curling over waistbands
barely contained?
What is it doing there?
The things underneath are after me:

**

they want in,
they want to go in,
and once in, they will never—
like a fish hook, with a barb—
come out again.
Yet by this passionate device
it is intended
that I sacrifice
my life.

II
And must it be beneath
a veil of white, a bride
like Iphegenia— all a-flutter—
not understanding
the nature of the knife?
Something will go in, poor girl.
It hardly matters if it's steel
or the recondite flesh
or which man it is
with a thing in his hand
which he points at your chest
and then—at the last second—
deflects beneath
the shrouds of your hem.
Your destiny is written in
the stars: you are
a lamb. You are

**

delicious. You are
a sacrifice.

III
The essence of escape
is in concealment. Yes,
my veil is white. Yes,
yes, I will vow a vow
for life, and none will doubt
the fullness of my
sacrifice. My man is
big; the biggest man
there is. And the stars
sing with delight
at my destiny—
I'm getting married—
to the ideal man.
He has no thing.
He wants no thing
from me. His verbs are
love and sacrifice
but his nouns
are remote as the heavens,
the sound of beating wings—
Oh, God!
I got away!
And all that is expected
of this bride
is that she pray.

POSTULANT

The others in my class
look sharp, glittering with sacred fire—
a passel of Marys wearing
the bugle beads of grace—
while I look blurred,
as though the photographer
put his thumb on my face
as the photo brewed in its chemical vat.
I was sick, I recall, my lungs full of fluid,
all my holes streaming mucous
and blood. But who listens
to the protest of the cells?
I was determined past the augury of pain
to enter my cell and lock myself up.
The others in my class look ecstatic,
tapped by the annunciating angel,
Gabriel, with his flower-wand
and manacles.
Let it be unto me,
their sequined faces say,
according to thy will,
while I have the widening eyes
of one paralyzed in the headlights
of a juggernaut.
My mouth is an O of surprise,
as if to say: I knew I had to die
but—like the corpse who saw it coming—
Why me? And why so young?

SMOKE OFFERING

My sister in Christ and I would hide
behind the guest house and smoke cigarettes,
clouds rising like incense, staining our breaths.
We would gargle in our cells and flap our habits
out the window to mask the smell. We would tell
each other stories of boyfriends and abortions
to remind ourselves of our bodies.
I went from Benson and Hedges Menthol Lights
to Marlboro Filters to Pall Mall, inhaling deeper
all the time. I longed for Gauloises or
hashish, a meerschaum pipe, and a ten-inch
cigarette holder to clamp between my teeth;
for Thai Gold in a hubbly-bubbly
and an opium pipe, for pot in a Power-Hitter.
I wanted to cram my nose with snuff
and to stuff my my cheeks
with chaw, as if all life
were reduced to mucous membranes
and bronchial tubes.
I wanted to spit tobacco juice
into a brass spittoon and make it ring
like the Angelus.

YESHUA REBUKED THE WAVES

on the sea of Galilee. They pleaded
with him to use his power in a way
they understood. He heard the plea, though
disappointed, sleepy,
like a flower furled in the bow,
unfurled too early he stepped out of sleep,
spoke to the gale:
    Silence! Be still. As if to say:
    the days will go on—rolling toward you
    in waves, one stout-hearted,
    hopeful day after another.
The storm decays and dies.
In the calm they feel a lack of him,
as if he, too, died down. His face is hid
from his disciples. They gape
at his back, astonished that this alien
materialized: *God forbid!* they whisper.
    His loosened power
    might pull the world apart—
    might shatter us!
Yeshua knows they're afraid of everything;
even their bright rabbi, sparkling
in the dripping aftermath. They want
the comprehensible.
They want the storm back.

HABIT

It descends with the Holy Spirit over
your face, breasts, legs, draping
the flesh in modesty, a falling curtain
of grace, and you: an empty dress-shape
with a scapular, a cincture, and a veil,
receptacle of God's will.
         Unless, of course, your body
is a swamp of desire, your heart
a simmering kettle, its shriek
clamped behind the grinding
and the grinding of your teeth.
Then your habit is a white enameled stove,
and you a roasting crackling pig inside,
on whom time will work the inevitable:
an implosion of self-immolation, or the blast outside.
And you: a projectile trailing the shreds of habit,
flames of rage and hunger your
contrail into the world.

WHAT YOU HAVE

A crucifix on a bare wall. Crocheted cincture
with a lover's knot tied at each end, which swing
as you walk (also known as "nun's balls"). The veil, with
or without wimple. Crepe-soled lace-up oxfords, black,
or sandals, preferably Dr. Scholl's. A watch,
plain, and your pectoral cross on a black string—small
enamel for annual vows, ebony for
perpetual. Your breviary with home made
cover from fabric out of common-stock. Gros-grain
bookmarks: anchor, heart, and cross. Your prayer list, tidy
and alphabetical when young, fragmented, much
amended when old (having been at it so long).
Underwear: invariably white cotton, though
colors have been seen among the postulants. Night-
gowns ornate, though some sleep nude in the sight of God.
A plain gold wedding ring—your mother's or your own.
A plot of earth by the chapel near the apple
orchard. Your constant mind. Your viscera. Your bones.

I KNOW I AM CAPABLE OF GREAT LOVE

I know it is the turbulence underground, of roots at war, spores escaping
into air. I know these battles occur on the white meadow of our beds.
Everything is troubled by combat.

I know it is death walking through the evergreens, an old man
in a straw hat. I know he must arrive at his destination, however slowly.
Everything is sharper in his gaze.

I know it is holding an old woman's hand, who has been held
but rarely. I know it is myself in the gray coil of her hair.
Every moment is eternal, leaning on her cane.

I move in the oxygen of passion: it heaves around me. The sky is a lung,
the bubbling earth is another lung. But I am unmoved.

I know I am capable of great love. My breasts are loam, my legs are
stems and roots. My hair turns red like the leaves, and will fall.

No gushing fountain, no, nor sprouting limb. My love is the moose
who steps carefully on a bed of pine needles, dappled flanks in the
shadows. I was there, then I was not there.

I know I am capable of great love. My love walks pensively through
evergreens. I know it must arrive, however slowly.

WHY I TURNED ONTO IRON GOAT ROAD

I drive down to Seattle
on the Wenatchee Mountain road.
The radio plays Glück's *Orfeo ed Euridice*—
the Dance of the Blessed Spirits.
Serenity embraces me on Cascade switchbacks
as blessed souls dance in the eternal circle of light.
Redeemed, I sigh, winding down the highway.
          But descending, the signal breaks up—
news intrudes. Every turn west brings a devilish
voice: Death! Calamity! Ruinous war!
Old Mephisto, even here on a mountain road,
flings his rocks of woe.
          But then, around the next bend, music
returns, the blessed souls hold hands again, dance
in a circle. And so I turn, the first chance I get,
off the highway onto Iron Goat Road, idled,
to catch the last notes of Glück
in the green-scented quiet
of a conifer woods.

ANNUNCIATION

I

In the Cortona fresco, her complexion is fair:
sapphire eyes, topaz hair—the face of a courteous girl.
Her nimbus is a crystal wedding plate.
The Evangelist says the angel's name is Gabriel:
God is Power.
Angelico gives him impetuous wings
flung up behind him like exclamations.
His lily hands point in two directions:
the left up to heaven,
the right at the heart of the girl.
His nimbus is a golden coin.
They lean in to each other. The archangel whispers
Father, heir, favor.
The virgin's face says *Yes.*
Her hands form wings like a dove across her breast.

II

The Masters tell this story in infinite versions:
her face expresses fear, or confidence, or shame.
His head is bowed, he kneels, or levitates on a cloud.
He is humble. He radiates power. She trembles. Her face
is serene. He holds out a palm frond, an olive branch, a scepter.
Her hands are folded, hold a lily, a rose,
a little book of psalms. Or else the book is on her knee,
has tumbled to the floor. He finds her in a cloister,
a gothic niche, a bower. The sky is empty,
with a moon, full of stars, or clouds of angels each
with a golden coin. Or a bust of the Heavenly Father floats

**

99

with the Holy Spirit amid ribbons of scripture:
Hail or *Ave, Miriam!*
Mary! Maria!
The one filled with willingness, charm, or finesse.

III
Inside the reliquary of devotion
is a girl threatened with disgrace, hustled
into marriage. No festivities for her!
The necessary courage: live with a black mark
against the family tree, seem normal in the
tsk and *alack* of community,
regain esteem, be truly married to the man
who takes you in the woe of isolation
and so learn to mother
the one who doesn't know
and cannot care, at least in infancy,
how he got there.

SHARON CUMBERLAND is the Director of the Creative Writing Program at Seattle University and an Associate Professor of English. Born and raised in the Episcopal Church, she lived at the Catholic Worker in New York City for one year and was a member of the Episcopal Order of Saint Helena for three years. After a career in New York as an arts manager at the Lincoln Center Theater Company and the Metropolitan Opera, she taught at Brooklyn Technical High School while earning a Ph.D. in English from the City University of New York. Her poetry has appeared in many journals including *Ploughshares*, *The Iowa Review*, *Verse*, and *Image*. She won Kalliope's Sue Saniel Elkind Award, The Pacific Northwest Writer's Association's Zola Award for Poetry, and the Writers Haven Press Bright Side Award. She was a Writer in Residence at the Jack Straw Foundation in 2007 and in 2010 at The Seasons Music Festival in Yakima, Washington. She has been guest at Yaddo, in Saratoga Springs, New York, for many years.